Svetlana Malysheva

Magnificent birds

coloring book

Hummingbirds
Mountain Bluebird
Cuban Tody
Atlantic Canary
Toco Toucan
Lovebirds
Mandarin Duck
Red-billed Firefinch
Resplendent Quetzal
Greenfinch
Purple Honeycreeper
Horned Sungem
Hornbill
Indian Peafowl
Kingfishers
Gouldian Finches
Owls
Northern Cardinals
Bird Of Paradise
African Golden Oriole
Atlantic Puffin
Hoopoe
Long-tailed Widowbird
Flamingo
Scarlet Macaw

Hummingbirds

Mountain Bluebird

Cuban Tody

Atlantic Canary

Toco Toucan

Lovebirds

Mandarin Duck

Red-billed Firefinch

Resplendent Quetzal

Toco Toucan

Greenfinch

Purple Honeycreeper

Horned Sungem

Hornbill

Indian Peafowl

Kingfishers

Gouldian Finches

Indian Peafowl

Owls

Northern Cardinals

Bird Of Paradise and African Golden Oriole

Atlantic Puffins

Hummingbird

Hoopoe

Purple Honeycreeper

Long-tailed Widowbird

Scarlet Macaw

Flamingo

Indian Peafowl

www.ingramcontent.com/pod-product-compliance
Lightning Source LLC
Chambersburg PA
CBHW081853280526

45789CB00007B/2688